James Madison
Founding Father

Lynn George

Rosen
REAL
READERS

om Books & Materials
New York

Published in 2003 by The Rosen Publishing Group, Inc.
29 East 21st Street, New York, NY 10010

Book Design: Haley Wilson

Photo Credits: Cover, pp. 1, 4, 8–9, 14 © North Wind Pictures; pp. 7, 12 © Corbis; p. 10 © Archive Photos.

ISBN: 0-8239-6382-9
6-pack ISBN: 0-8239-9564-X

Manufactured in the United States of America

Contents

James Madison was born on March 16, 1751, in the **colony** of Virginia. James was an excellent student and loved to learn. He also loved **freedom** and believed there could be no freedom without knowledge.

Madison finished school in 1771. Three years later, he became a government leader.

Madison tried to set up a public school system to teach both women and men. He believed all people had the right to learn.

The Colonies Fight for Freedom

In 1775, the colonies began their fight for freedom from England in a war called the **American Revolution**. In 1776, Madison helped the people of Virginia write a statement of their rights. Congress put many of these same ideas into a statement for all the colonies called the **Declaration of Independence**.

The Declaration of Independence was adopted on July 4, 1776.

IN CONGRESS, JULY 4, 1776.

The unanimous Declaration of the thirteen united States of America.

New Laws for a New Nation

The colonies won the American Revolution in 1783 and formed the United States of America. From 1784 to 1786, Madison helped to make laws for Virginia. He tried to end the terrible system of **slavery**, but could not.

In 1787, Madison and other leaders met to write our **Constitution** (kahn-stuh-TOO-shun), a system of rules that our country still uses today.

Madison did so much to shape the Constitution that he was called the "Father of the Constitution."

Congress OF THE United States,

begun and held at the City of New-York, on
Wednesday the fourth of March, one thousand seven hundred and eighty-nine.

THE Conventions of a number of the States, having at the time of their adopting the Constitution, expressed a desire, in order to prevent misconstruction or abuse of its powers, that further declaratory and restrictive clauses should be added: And as extending the ground of public confidence in the Government, will best ensure the beneficent ends of its institution.

RESOLVED by the Senate and House of Representatives of the United States of America, in Congress assembled, two thirds of both Houses concurring, that the following Articles be proposed to the Legislatures of the several States, as amendments to the Constitution of the United States, all, or any of which Articles, when ratified by three fourths of the said Legislatures, to be valid to all intents and purposes, as part of the said Constitution; viz.

ARTICLES in addition to, and amendment of the Constitution of the United States of America, proposed by Congress, and ratified by the Legislatures of the several States, pursuant to the fifth Article of the original Constitution.

Article the first. ... After the first enumeration required by the first Article of the Constitution, there shall be one Representative for every thirty thousand, until the number shall amount to one hundred, after which, the proportion shall be so regulated by Congress, that there shall be not less than one hundred Representatives, nor less than one Representative for every forty thousand persons, until the number of Representatives shall amount to two hundred, after which the proportion shall be so regulated by Congress, that there shall not be less than two hundred Representatives, nor more than one Representative for every fifty thousand persons.

Article the second. ... No law, varying the compensation for the services of the Senators and Representatives, shall take effect, until an election of Representatives shall have intervened.

Article the third. ... Congress shall make no law respecting an establishment of religion, or prohibiting the free exercise thereof; or abridging the freedom of speech, or of the press; or the right of the people peaceably to assemble, and to petition the Government for a redress of grievances.

Article the fourth. ... A well regulated militia, being necessary to the security of a free State, the right of the people to keep and bear arms, shall not be infringed.

Article the fifth. ... No soldier shall, in time of peace be quartered in any house, without the consent of the owner, nor in time of war, but in a manner to be prescribed by law.

Article the sixth. ... The right of the people to be secure in their persons, houses, papers, and effects, against unreasonable searches and seizures, shall not be violated, and no warrants shall issue, but upon probable cause, supported by oath or affirmation, and particularly describing the place to be searched, and the persons or things to be seized.

Article the seventh. ... No person shall be held to answer for a capital, or otherwise infamous crime, unless on a presentment or indictment of a Grand jury, except in cases arising in the land or naval forces, or in the Militia, when in actual service in time of war or public danger; nor shall any person be subject for the same offence to be twice put in jeopardy of life or limb; nor shall be compelled in any criminal case to be a witness against himself, nor be deprived of life, liberty, or property, without due process of law; nor shall private property be taken for public use, without just compensation.

Article the eighth. ... In all criminal prosecutions, the accused shall enjoy the right to a speedy and public trial, by an impartial jury of the State and district wherein the crime shall have been committed, which district shall have been previously ascertained by law, and to be informed of the nature and cause of the accusation; to be confronted with the witnesses against him; to have compulsory process for obtaining witnesses in his favor, and to have the assistance of counsel for his defence.

Article the ninth. ... In suits at common law, where the value in controversy shall exceed twenty dollars, the right of trial by jury shall be preserved, and no fact tried by a jury, shall be otherwise re-examined in any court of the United States, than according to the rules of the common law.

Article the tenth. ... Excessive bail shall not be required, nor excessive fines imposed, nor cruel and unusual punishments inflicted.

Article the eleventh. ... The enumeration in the Constitution, of certain rights, shall not be construed to deny or disparage others retained by the people.

Article the twelfth. ... The powers not delegated to the United States by the Constitution, nor prohibited by it to the States, are reserved to the States respectively, or to the people.

Frederick Augustus Muhlenberg, Speaker of the House of Representatives.

John Adams, Vice-President of the United States, and President of the Senate.

ATTEST,

John Beckley, Clerk of the House of Representatives.

Sam. A. Otis, Secretary of the Senate.

10

Guarding Freedom

In 1788, Madison helped Congress write the **Bill of Rights**, which lists freedoms the government cannot take away from the people. When President John Adams and Congress made a law that took away **free speech** in 1798, Madison objected. He wrote that a government run by the people needs free speech. The law ended in 1801, but it had made people angry at President Adams.

The Bill of Rights is one of the most important things ever written in American history. It lists every person's basic rights.

Helping to Lead the Nation

In 1801, Thomas Jefferson became our third president. President Jefferson asked Madison to help him lead the nation. For eight years, Madison carried out many important duties for President Jefferson. He helped President Jefferson buy a lot of land from France. This made the United States two times as large as it had been.

Jefferson wrote that his friend Madison was a leader of great honor and wisdom.

13

In 1809, Madison became our fourth president. He served for eight years. It was an unhappy time. There were disagreements with other countries and another war with England.

In 1817, Madison returned to his farm in Virginia. He helped Jefferson start the **University** of Virginia. Madison's love of learning stayed with him until he died in 1836.

Glossary

American Revolution A war the American colonies fought from 1775 to 1783 to win their freedom from England.

Bill of Rights The first ten statements added to the Constitution, which list rights the government cannot take away from the people.

colony Land that has been settled by people who live in one country but are ruled by another.

Constitution A system of rules that tells the powers of the government and the rights of the people.

Declaration of Independence A statement of the colonists' rights and their reasons for going to war to win their freedom from England.

freedom The power to do, say, or think what you believe.

free speech The right to say what you believe.

slavery The unfair system of being "owned" and having to work for someone else. Rich landowners forced Africans to work on their farms.

university A school where people can study to become a doctor, a teacher, a government leader, and so forth.

Index